KU-180-612

19. MAR 04

10. JUN 05

05. SEP 05

10. MAY 06

12. JUN 06

30. SEP 06

06. MAR 07

03 APR 07

09. MAR 10.

1 3 MAY 2013

WITHDRAWN

CORNHILL LIBRARY
Tel: 696209

....

**PLEASE RETURN TO THE ABOVE LIBRARY OR ANY OTHER ABERDEEN
CITY LIBRARY, ON OR BEFORE THE DUE DATE. TO RENEW, PLEASE
QUOTE THE DUE DATE AND THE BARCODE NUMBER.**

Aberdeen City Council
Library & Information Services

ABERDEEN CITY LIBRARIES

FRANCE

LETTERS FROM AROUND THE WORLD

Teresa Fisher

Photographs by Andy Johnstone

CHERRYTREE BOOKS

Titles in this series

BANGLADESH • BRAZIL • CHINA • FRANCE • INDIA • ITALY • JAMAICA • JAPAN • KENYA • SPAIN

A Cherrytree Book

Conceived and produced by

Nutshell
MEDIA

Intergen House
65-67 Western Road
Hove BN3 2JQ, UK
www.nutshellmedialtd.co.uk

First published in 2003 by
Evans Brothers Ltd
2A Portman Mansions
Chiltern Street
London W1U 6NR

VISIT OUR WEBSITE
www.evansbooks.co.uk

© Copyright Evans Brothers 2003

Editor: Polly Goodman
Designer: Tim Mayer
Map artwork: Encompass Graphics Ltd
All other artwork: Tim Mayer
Geography consultant: Jeff Stanfield, Geography
   Inspector for Ofsted
Literacy consultant: Anne Spiring

Picture acknowledgements
All photographs were taken by Andy Johnstone
except: p26 (bottom) Britstock (Yashiro Haga);
p28 (Eiffel Tower) Dorian Shaw.

Printed in Hong Kong

914.4

Acknowledgements
The photographer would like to thank Yvonne, Patrick,
Victor and Germain Calsou, and the staff of Jules Julien
School, Toulouse, for all their help with this book.

All Rights Reserved. No part of this publication may be
reproduced, stored in a retrieval system or transmitted
in any form, electronic, mechanical, photocopying,
recording or otherwise, without prior permission of
Evans Brothers Limited.

British Library Cataloguing in Publication Data
   Fisher, Teresa
   France – (Letters From Around the World)
   1. France - Social conditions - 1995 - Juvenile
   literature
   2. France - Social life and customs - 1995 -
   Juvenile literature
   I. Title
   944'.084

ISBN 184234143X

Cover: Victor and friends in front of the River Garonne.
Title Page: Victor in the school playground.
This page: The peaks of the Pyrenees mountains.
Contents page: Victor carrying a freshly baked baguette
home for breakfast.
Glossary page: Victor reads a favourite book, *The Magic
Spuds*, in his bedroom.
Further Information page: People dressed up for the
Mardi Gras celebrations in Toulouse.
Index: One of the many bridges over the River Garonne.

Contents

My Country

Wednesday, 9 January

46 Avenue des Avions
42703 Toulouse
France

Dear Jo,

Bonjour! (You say 'bonj-or'. This means 'hello' in French.)

My name's Victor Calsou. I'm 9 years old. I live in Toulouse, a big city in the south of France. Look on the map to find Toulouse. I've got an older brother called Germain, who's 10.

It's great to be your pen-friend. I'll be able to help you with class projects on France.

Write back soon!

From

Victor

This is my family on a bike ride. I'm the one in the middle. Do you have a bike?

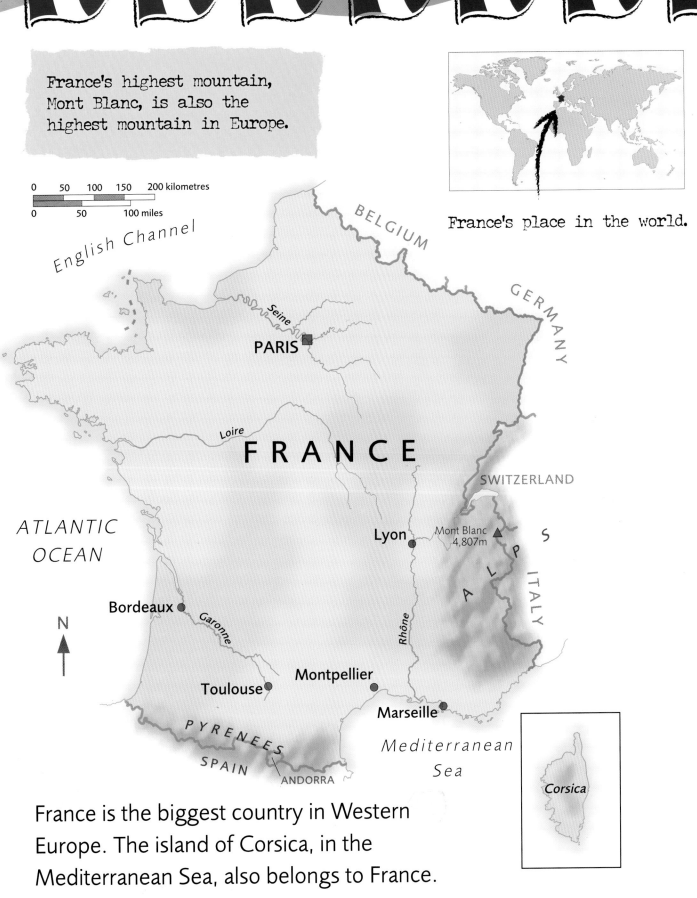

France's highest mountain, Mont Blanc, is also the highest mountain in Europe.

France's place in the world.

0   50   100   150   200 kilometres

0   50   100 miles

English Channel

BELGIUM

GERMANY

Seine

PARIS

Loire

FRANCE

SWITZERLAND

ATLANTIC
OCEAN

Lyon

Mont Blanc
4,807m

A L P S

ITALY

N

Bordeaux

Garonne

Rhône

Montpellier

Toulouse

Marseille

PYRENEES

Mediterranean
Sea

SPAIN

ANDORRA

Corsica

France is the biggest country in Western Europe. The island of Corsica, in the Mediterranean Sea, also belongs to France.

Most people in France live in big towns and cities near the coast or, like Toulouse, by a river. Toulouse is the fourth-largest city in France. Over half a million people live there.

The city is famous for making aircraft and space rockets. Toulouse University is the second-biggest university in France after Paris.

The Garonne river flows through the centre of Toulouse.

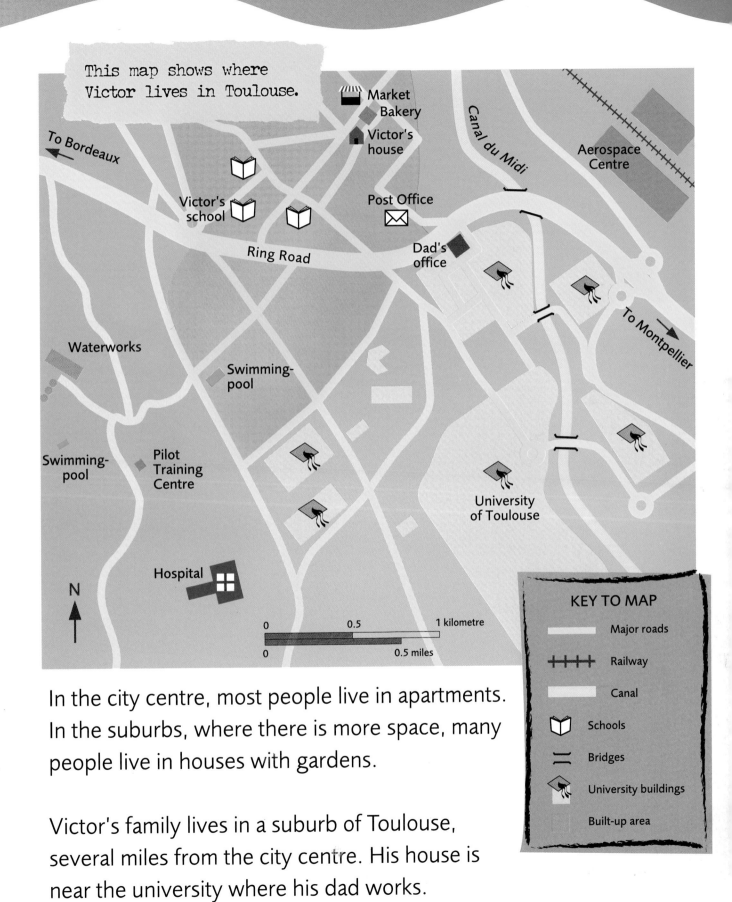

This map shows where Victor lives in Toulouse.

Market
Bakery
Victor's house
To Bordeaux
Victor's school
Post Office
Canal du Midi
Aerospace Centre
Ring Road
Dad's office
To Montpellier
Waterworks
Swimming-pool
Swimming-pool
Pilot Training Centre
University of Toulouse
Hospital
N

| 0 | 0.5 | 1 kilometre |
| 0 | | 0.5 miles |

KEY TO MAP

Major roads

Railway

Canal

Schools

Bridges

University buildings

Built-up area

In the city centre, most people live in apartments. In the suburbs, where there is more space, many people live in houses with gardens.

Victor's family lives in a suburb of Toulouse, several miles from the city centre. His house is near the university where his dad works.

Landscape and Weather

Toulouse is surrounded by rolling farmland and vineyards. To the south are the Pyrenees mountains. To the south-east, the sandy beaches of the Mediterranean Sea are just two hours away by car.

The Pyrenees are covered by snow in the winter. People go there to ski.

The climate in the south of France is hotter and drier than in the north. Summers in Toulouse are long and dry – ideal for growing grapes.

Toulouse's Climate

January	July
Temperature	**Temperature**
7°C	23°C
65mm	45mm
Rainfall	**Rainfall**

Flowers grow well in Toulouse's hot summer climate. Sunflower seeds are used to make sunflower oil.

At Home

Victor's family lives in a traditional-style house with a small garden. The windows have wooden shutters, which are closed in the summer to keep the house cool. They are also shut at night.

Victor and his family outside their house, with their cat, Saphir. *Saphir* is French for 'Sapphire'.

On the ground floor there is a large living room, where the family watches television and listens to the hi-fi. They have a separate dining room and a kitchen.

Upstairs there is a bathroom and three bedrooms. There is also a study, where Victor's dad sometimes works on the computer.

The Calsou family has seven television channels to choose from.

Victor does his homework in his bedroom and reads his favourite books there.

11

Victor often helps his
mum in the kitchen. The
dishwasher helps with
the washing-up.

Victor and Germain have to help with the housework and keep their bedrooms tidy. Sometimes they help do the gardening, or wash the family's two cars. But it is much more fun playing with their toys.

Victor and Germain love
playing with building sets.

Thursday, 14 March

46 Avenue des Avions
42703 Toulouse
France

Bonjour Jo!

Thanks for your letter last week. Did I tell you that it was Germain's birthday yesterday? He was 11. After school, his best friend Etienne came home for tea. Mum made our favourite cake – a very sticky almond tart. Delicious!

Then we played with Germain's presents. He got a new bicycle from Mum and Dad. I gave him some marbles. When's your birthday? Write back and tell me – mine's in May.

From
Victor

Germain always tries to get the biggest piece of tart!

Food and Mealtimes

On school days Victor wakes up at 7 a.m. For breakfast he has hot chocolate and croissants, or crusty bread with jam. Sometimes he has cereal with milk. There is always bread with every meal. The bread is usually long, thin loaves, called baguettes.

Every morning, Victor and Germain buy fresh baguettes and croissants from the local bakery.

There are over 365 different
French cheeses — one for
every day of the year!

The main meal of the day is usually
the evening dinner, which all the
family eat together. Often there
are four courses – a starter, a meat
or fish dish with vegetables, then
cheese, followed by dessert.

Victor drinks his hot chocolate
from a bowl, which is the
custom in France.

Once a week, Victor's parents buy fresh fruit and vegetables from the local market.

Victor loves food, especially cheese, pâté and oysters, which are typical French dishes. One French dish that he does not like is snails with garlic butter, but his mum and dad think they are delicious.

Every region in France has its own local dishes. Sausages and salami are specialities in Toulouse.

Sunday, 4 May

46 Avenue des Avions

42703 Toulouse

France

Hi Jo,

Thanks for the recipe you sent last week. Here's one for you.
It's for my favourite dessert – crêpes.

You will need: 250g flour, a little salt, 2 eggs, $^1/2$ litre milk,
40g melted butter, jam, or sugar and lemon juice.

1. Add the eggs, milk, melted butter and salt slowly to the flour and
   whisk everything together until it's smooth. Leave for one hour.
2. Pour a little of the mixture into a hot, greased frying pan and cook
   quickly over a high heat until the bottom of the crêpe is golden.
   (Mum always does that bit for me.)
3. Flip the crêpe over, cook the other side and put it on a plate.
4. Spread a little jam, or sugar and lemon juice, on to the crêpe.
   Roll it up and serve immediately.

I hope you like them!

From
Victor

Here I am breaking
the eggs.

School Day

Victor and Germain go to the local primary school, just ten minutes' walk from their home. If it is raining, their dad takes them in his car. Like most French schoolchildren, they do not wear a school uniform.

Victor and Germain always cross the road at the zebra crossing on their way to school.

Victor uses a writing board in maths lessons. The board can be wiped clean to write new sums.

Lessons start at 8.30 a.m. and end at 4.30 p.m, with a two-hour lunch-break in the middle of the day.

There are 25 children in Victor's class. They study French, English, maths, geography, history and science, all with the same class teacher.

Victor has lunch every day in the school canteen. Some of his friends go home for lunch.

During the lunch-
break, Victor plays
marbles in the school
playground.

In France, children start
school at the age of 6.
Victor will stay at primary
school until he is 11. Then
he will go to secondary
school. After that he
hopes to go to university.

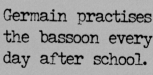

Germain practises
the bassoon every
day after school.

Friday 19 July

46 Avenue des Avions
42703 Toulouse
France

Bonjour Jo!

I'm glad you liked the crêpes. I prefer them with jam, too.

Did I tell you that in France we don't have lessons on Wednesday afternoons? It gives us time to do other things like sport, painting, music, or drama at the local youth club.

My favourite sport's football. I also like wood carving. I go to a wood-carving club every Wednesday. Germain belongs to a rugby club. Do you belong to any clubs or teams?

From

Victor

These are some of Germain's friends playing rugby in their after-school club.

Off to Work

Victor's dad is a biology researcher at Toulouse University. His mum helps local schools to plan their lessons. Both parents start work at 8.30 a.m. They travel to work in their cars.

Victor's dad is doing an experiment in the laboratory.

This waiter works in a busy café in Toulouse.

There are lots of different types of work in Toulouse. Some people work in banks, shops or companies. Others work in factories. Outside the city, farmers grow crops and raise animals.

This man is a goat farmer. He uses goat's milk to make delicious cheeses.

Free Time

Victor spends his free time drawing, painting, reading, playing with his toys and watching television. He loves playing football with his friends, going to the cinema, or swimming at the local pool.

Everyone enjoys meeting friends in cafés in France.

At the weekend, Victor often goes on a bike ride with his family. In the school holidays, they go walking in the Pyrenees mountains. Sometimes they visit England.

Victor's brother Germain plays with his diabolo. He throws it in the air and then catches it on the string.

The cycle path along the river is great for bike rides.

Religion and Festivals

These children are dressed up for a local festival in France.

Most people in France are Roman Catholic, but there are other religions, too, including Islam and Judaism.

Christmas and Easter are the most important Roman Catholic festivals. Forty days before Easter, there is an exciting carnival called Mardi Gras in Toulouse.

At Mardi Gras, everyone dresses up for a big night-time procession.

Tuesday, 23 December

46 Avenue des Avions
42703 Toulouse
France

Hi Jo,

I'm really excited because tomorrow it's Christmas Eve. Do you celebrate Christmas, too?

I've been decorating the house with tinsel. Tomorrow we'll have a big meal with my grandparents and give out presents. I'm hoping for a new bike. Then we'll go to church for a special service at midnight. It's great being awake at midnight.

Joyeux Noël! (This means 'Happy Christmas' in French.)

From

Victor

This is me decorating the Christmas tree. It's not a real tree so we can use it again every year.

Fact File

Capital city: Paris is the capital of France. It has many famous museums, art galleries and buildings, including the Eiffel Tower. Visitors can take a lift to the top or they can climb the 1,652 steps instead! On a clear day you can see for up to 70km from the top of the tower.

Language: French is the official language of France and of another 21 countries in the world.

Flag: The French flag is called the *tricolore*, which means 'three-coloured'. Red and blue represent the city of Paris and white is the traditional colour for French kings.

Highest mountain: Mont Blanc (4,807m). This is in the Alps, in south-east France.

Longest river: The Loire (1,020km). It flows from the middle of France to the Atlantic Ocean.

Famous products: France is famous for its cars, aircraft and perfume, and for its fashions, fine cooking and wines. The most famous wine is a fizzy white wine called champagne.

Fastest trains: French trains (called TGV) are the fastest in the world. They reach speeds of up to 300kph.

Currency: The euro (€). This replaced French francs in January 2002. There are 100 cents in a euro. It is now the currency used by 12 out of the 15 member countries of the European Union.

Famous people:
Napoleon Bonaparte was an army general who became Emperor of France in 1804. Claude Monet (born in 1840) was a painter who led the Impressionist movement. Charles Perrault (born in 1628) wrote the fairy tales *Sleeping Beauty*, *Little Red Riding Hood* and *Cinderella*.

Festivals: There are over 400 festivals in France. The biggest is called Bastille Day on 14 July. Many are religious festivals, such as Purim (above), Christmas and Easter.

Tourism: More people visit France for their holidays than any other country in Europe. One of the biggest attractions for children is Disneyland, in Paris.

Stamps: Most French stamps are fairly plain, but sometimes they have pictures or cartoons on them.

ABERDEEN CITY LIBRARIES

Glossary

apartment A flat, or group of rooms to live in.

baguettes (You say 'bag-et') Crusty bread, shaped like long, thin sticks.

bonjour! This means 'hello' or 'good day' in French.

carnival A big festival with music and dancing.

Christmas The birthday of Jesus Christ.

crêpes (You say 'crep') Thin, round pancakes, served with either a sweet or a savoury filling.

croissants (You say 'kwa-son') A rich, buttery pastry shaped like a half-moon, often eaten at breakfast.

Easter A Christian festival when people remember Jesus rising from the dead.

European Union A group of 15 countries in Europe that work and trade together.

Joyeux Noël! This means 'Happy Christmas' in French.

pâté (You say 'pattay') A tasty meat paste, usually eaten with bread.

researcher Someone who makes careful investigations to find out new facts.

Roman Catholic A member of the Roman Catholic Church, the largest branch of Christianity. The head of this church is the Pope.

saint A title given to holy people by some Christian churches.

shutters Wooden, slatted doors attached to the outside of glass windows. They help keep houses cool in hot climates.

suburb A small district at the edge of a town or city.

Further Information

Information books:

A Flavour of France by Teresa Fisher (Hodder Wayland, 1998)

Country Insights: France by Teresa Fisher (Hodder Wayland, 1997)

Fiesta! France by Charles Phillips (Franklin Watts, 1998)

Picture a Country: France by Henry Pluckrose (Franklin Watts, 1998)

Step into France by Fred Martin (Heinemann, 1998)

A Visit to France by Rob Alcraft (Heinemann, 1999)

We Come from France by Teresa Fisher (Hodder Wayland, 1999)

A World of Recipes: France by Sue Townsend (Heinemann, 2002)

Fiction:

Degas and the Little Dancer, A story of Edgar Degas by Laurence Anholt (Frances Lincoln, 1995)

The Little Prince by Antoine de St Exupéry

Resource Packs:

Un, Deux, Trois: First French Rhymes (Frances Lincoln, 1996)
A selection of French nursery rhymes for young children, including an audio-cassette.

Websites:

CIA Factbook
www.cia.gov/cia/publications/factbook/
Basic facts and figures about France and other countries.

French Tourist Office
www.franceguide.com/

Index